Praise for *101 Tips to Lighten Your Burden*

"Jennifer Bonn writes in a lighthearted knowledgeable manner, making me want to read the next bit of wisdom before I lay down the last. I always walk away with a warm heart and smile that are triggered by her thoughtful words and positive spin on life. I love that she makes me think about how I am choosing to live life, her words are easy, truthful and challenging in a good way."
Schelli Hutchinson, educator

"There is no doubt that Jennifer Bonn's new book will meet your expectations. I have been following her writing for years, and her essays are always insightful and intriguing and often humorous. Jennifer's writing has a way of empowering you. It is a feel good guide of learning, accepting, and discovering."
Kimberly Tucker, aircraft mechanic

"Over the years I have read many excellent common sense editorials written by Jennifer Bonn in newspapers and magazines. I am so happy that she has decided to compile them in this book. She is an inspiration to not only her students but to anyone looking for down to earth guidance for themselves and their children. Every family should have a copy of this book at home. It helps prepare anyone to face the challenges of growing up and life in general."
Doug Sucher , 1st Lt. U.S. Army (retired), advisory board member for the YMCA in Cobb County

"I had the pleasure and honor of editing this book for Jennifer Bonn. She is a teacher of 40 years' experience, who shares all the wisdom she has acquired. Her students were lucky people, and I am sure she had a major influence in improving hundreds of lives. In this book, she gives you an opportunity to also receive the same benefit.

I have a Ph.D. in psychology, and decades of therapeutic experience, and I can tell you, this book could have been written by an experienced psychologist. Ms. Bonn could change professions, and become a professor in the psychology department of any university. In particular, she is an expert in positive psychology.

In fact, my latest book is *From Depression to Contentment*, and I was amazed to find a great many of my recommendations in Ms. Bonn's delightful book."

Bob Rich, PhD, Wombat Hollow, Australia

"Jennifer Bonn's writings are inspiring and thought provoking. Her articles contain positive steps to become a better person. Her writings always contain sound advice with a slightly humorous slant."

Rebecca Gilbert, Director, Physician Coding Compliance,
Wellstar Health System

101 TIPS

TO LIGHTEN YOUR BURDEN

PRACTICAL ADVICE *for* LIFE

JENNIFER BONN

Loving Healing Press

Ann Arbor * Milton-Keynes

101 Tips To Lighten Your Burden: Practical Advice For Life
Copyright © 2022 by Jennifer Bonn. All Rights Reserved.

ISBN 978-1-61599-609-4 paperback
ISBN 978-1-61599-610-0 hardcover
ISBN 978-1-61599-611-7 ebook
Audiobook available from Audible.com and iTunes

Published by
Loving Healing Press
5145 Pontiac Trail
Ann Arbor, MI 48105

www.LHPress.com
info@LHPress.com
Tollfree 888-761-6268

Distributed by Ingram (USA/CAN/AU) and Bertrams Books (UK/EU)

Library of Congress Cataloging-in-Publication Data

Names: Bonn, Jennifer, 1958- author.
Title: 101 tips to lighten your burden : practical advice for life / Jennifer Bonn.
Other titles: One hundred one tips to lighten your burden
Description: Ann Arbor : Loving Healing Press, [2021] | Includes bibliographical references and index. | Summary: "We all have burdens of some kind, though we may carry them in different ways. The way we react to our challenges in life will determine whether we continue to struggle or whether we live life to the fullest. When we are faced with roadblocks in life, we always have choices. We can let them paralyze us and not move forward, we can bust through them leaving havoc in our wake, or we can find a way around them continuing down our path"-- Provided by publisher.
Identifiers: LCCN 2021050982 (print) | LCCN 2021050983 (ebook) | ISBN 9781615996094 (paperback) | ISBN 9781615996100 (hardcover) | ISBN 9781615996117 (ebook)
Subjects: LCSH: Conduct of life. | Self-realization.
Classification: LCC BJ1589 .B66 2021 (print) | LCC BJ1589 (ebook) | DDC 170/.44--dc23/eng/20211115
LC record available at https://lccn.loc.gov/2021050982
LC ebook record available at https://lccn.loc.gov/2021050983

Contents

Introduction 1
1. You Are Wonderfully Made. 1
2. Believe You Can. 1
3. Do Not Compare Yourself To Others. 1
4. Do Not Allow Anyone to Limit You. 2
5. Filter the Harmful Speech of Those People Who Have No Filter. 2
6. Don't Care About What Doesn't Matter. 3
7. Realize That the Ideals Society Gives to Us are Unrealistic. 3
8. Social Media Can Raise Our Anxiety Level and Change Our Self-perception. 3
9. Find The Knowledge You Need. 4
10. Separate Constructive Criticism from Negative Noise 4
11. Realize That You Have Special Gifts to Offer. 4
12. Seek Inspiration to Motivate You. 6
13. Replace Negative Self-Talk with Positive Words. 7
14. Find Your Crew. 7
15. Keep Improving. 7
16. Adopt a Strong Mindset. 8
17. Allow People to See Who You Are 8
18. When We Are Transparent Others Follow Our Lead. 9
19. Dare to be Different. 9
20. The Haters in Your Life Have Less Ammunition When You Admit Your Shortcomings. 9
21. People Are More Comfortable Around You When You Are Yourself. 10
22. Being Transparent Can Help You to Grow. 10
23. Communication Has to Go Both Ways to Be Effective. 10
24. Give Your Listener Your Undivided Attention. 11

25. When You Have a Conversation, Do Not Try to Top the Other Person's Troubles or Switch to a Story About You. 11

26. Ask Questions About What You Are Hearing. 11

27. Don't Allow Your Emotions to Control Your Words. 12

28. You Can Change Someone's World with Your Words. 12

29. Let Others into Your Space. 12

30. Relationships Should Be a Top Priority. 13

31. Time Is One of the Crucial Elements of a Good Relationship. 13

32. Show an Interest in the People in Your Circle. 14

33. Know That Friendship Should Be Quality Not Quantity. 14

34. Always Love Fully. 14

35. Sometimes You Must Let a Relationship Go. 15

36. It Is Important to Be Part of a Community. 15

37. Every Day You Have a Chance to Make a Connection. 15

38. Be a Mentor. 16

39. Do Acts of Kindness. 16

40. Be The Sail, Not the Anchor in a Relationship. 17

41. Any Relationship is a Give and Take. 17

42. Positive Attitudes Attract People to You. 18

43. Be Ready to Forgive. 18

44. Understand Before Reacting. 18

45. No one Has to Settle for Unhappiness. 19

46. There is Always Someone Else Who Has Bigger Problems Than You. 19

47. Make a List of What You Want from Life. 19

48. Have a Fearless Attitude. 20

49. Being Stressed and Overwhelmed Is a Choice. 20

50. Failure Has a Nasty Sting but It Makes You Stronger. 21

51. Accept That Most People Who Witnessed Your Failure Probably Moved on Five Minutes After It Happened So You Should Too. 22

52. A Good Sense of Humor is A Powerful Weapon to Yield Against Failure. 22

53. Breathe and Believe. 22

54. Take a Break 23

55. Set Reachable Goals. 23

56. Frustration Is A Waste Of Time. 23

57. Excuses Are Your Failure Safety Net. 24

58. Be Honest About What Went Wrong. 24

59. Be Open to New Possibilities. 24

60. We All Have Demons in Some Form. 25

61. Admit You Have a Demon. 25

62. Find The Support You Need. 25

63. Make The Necessary Changes. 26

64. Prayer is Powerful. 26

65. Be Thankful for Your Scars. 26

66. Our Health is a Factor in Every Area of Our Lives. 27

67. Find The Quiet. 27

68. Movement is a Must. 28

69. Music is a Healer. 28

70. Spending Time with Animals Is Good Therapy. 28

71. Cooking is a Healthy Pastime. 29

72. Practicing Gratitude is an Important Exercise in Healing. 29

73. Sleep Can Solve Many of Our Problems. 29

74. Disconnect to Connect. 30

75. Manage Stress. 30

76. Slow Down to Enjoy More. 30

77. Rest and Food Make All the Difference. 31

78. Know What Fuels You. 31

79. Learn From Everyone. 32

80. Laugh As Often as Possible. 32
81. Change Your Focus. 32
82. Don't Lose Your Mind. 33
83. It's Not That Hard to Make Friends. 34
84. Sharing What You Have Is Important. 34
85. There Must Be Time to Play. 34
86. The Toys We Have Do Not Ensure Happiness. 35
87. Take The Time to Wander and Wonder. 35
88. They Never Worry About Time. 35
89. What Needs to Be Thrown Out in The Trash? 36
90. How Can You Improve Your Health? 36
91. You Need to Surround Yourself with People Who Will Make You Better. 36
92. Learn to Say No. 36
93. Do What You Love. 37
94. Break Your Mold. 37
95. Imagine More. 37
96. Map Out Your Goals. 37
97. Make a vision board. 38
98. Ask God to open doors. 38
99. Nix Negativity. 38
100. Consistency Will Change Your Life. 39
101. God Will Send You Who and What You Need. 41
Conclusion 43
About the Author 45
Bibliography 47
Index 49

Introduction

One thing I know for sure is we all have burdens of some kind. Some of these burdens are mental and some are physical. Some have been fashioned by ourselves and others are the result of outside forces. We all carry the burdens in different ways. The way we react to our challenges in life will determine whether we continue to struggle or whether we live life to the fullest.

I would like to suggest some ideas about how to react to what you struggle with in life and how that can make all the difference for you. When we are faced with roadblocks in life we always have choices. We can let them paralyze us and not move forward, we can bust through them leaving havoc in our wake, or we can find a way around them continuing down our path.

This book gives you quick, easy to read advice on how to handle many of life's struggles. It is a book you can keep picking up when you need a lift. It will be like the voice of a friend telling you what you can do to make the situation better. I think the words will also help you on the days when the burden feels too heavy, and you need some words to soothe your mind.

I hope my words will help you because they are given with love. Pass the words on to others who need them and let's help each other to carry any burdens, to see the many blessings, and to lead the lives we deserve.

101 Tips to Lighten Your Burden

1. **You Are Wonderfully Made.**
   You may feel you don't fit in or you are not understood, but everyone has both faults and special qualities. You have unique elements that make you special, and you will find people who appreciate who you are, so do not try to be anything other than your true self. Your real friends are those who love you exactly as you are. Focus on those strengths that make you shine and improve on areas where you know you could be better. Find a mantra that states your value and say it over and over to yourself. Simple ones could be "I am worthy, I am strong, I am enough."

2. **Believe You Can.**
   Many of us suffer from insecurities, and we would rather avoid trying something new and failing at it than being stagnant with what is comfortable. We cannot grow until we step out of our comfort zone, but often that first step is terrifying. Positive thinking can send out strong energy and when you use positive words of affirmation, it is amazing to see the results. After you prove once or twice that you are capable of difficult tasks, you will gain confidence and continue to be stronger.

3. **Do Not Compare Yourself To Others.**
   We often see someone who we think has everything one could want in life, but underneath that mask of perfection are some elements that might not be very pretty. As you start to become acquainted with someone you perceive to be perfect, those elements usually rise to the surface. Be grateful for your blessings and realize that imperfection is more interesting and involves inspirational stories.

4. **Do Not Allow Anyone to Limit You.**
   If someone tells you that you cannot be who you want to be, or that a passion or dream is unrealistic, create a plan to prove them wrong. Even friends and family members can be negative about our aspirations, and often it is because they are worried about us being hurt. Find people who will be your cheerleaders and continue following what makes you happy. When I was forty-two, I had an overwhelming desire to have a third child. When I voiced this thought, reactions were always negative and included comments about my age at the time, how old I would be when my child graduated high school, and the potential for health problems because I was an older mother. I ignored the comments and had my daughter Kaitlyn who is the light of my life. I would have missed out on so much if I had listened to others.

5. **Filter the Harmful Speech of Those People Who Have No Filter.**
   People can say hurtful things often without being aware of what impact their words can have. I am amazed at some of the things people think it is ok to say. Although someone might not know what he is talking about, after you have been criticized enough, you begin to ask yourself if there is some truth in what the person is saying. We need to keep a running dialogue with ourselves to guard against these hateful comments made by people who want to feel better about themselves. We need to help each other have thicker skin for those comments and know how to respond. I have found that when you respond to a hurtful comment with laughter as if the comment was absurd, you can diffuse the moment. You can also ignore it and respond kindly since the person being hateful probably has issues much heavier than what he is claiming you have.

6. **Don't Care About What Doesn't Matter.**
There are days when you feel like you need to have mental armor because of your interactions with others. Learn to not react to hateful comments or empty actions. They do not matter, and you are strong enough to not let anything like that wound you. Don't continually beat yourself up wondering if you should have said something differently or reacted in another way. It's in the past, so it's time to move on to more important things.

7. **Realize That the Ideals Society Gives to Us are Unrealistic.**
We only must pick up a magazine to see what our ideal of beauty is and that perfection comes with a mental and physical price. We need to stop comparing ourselves to celebrities. Find your version of beautiful which is whatever makes you feel comfortable in your skin. One of the topics in my class was beauty and how it affects our lives. My students had to do a presentation on what their definition of beauty was and how it affected them. One girl gave all of us a mirror, (it was a class of all girls), and she said, "What is the first thing that comes to your mind?" Everyone started saying negative comments about themselves and the presenter said, "Why do we do that as women? Why can we not see our beauty?" I believe the answer to that is because we believe someone else's version of the ideal.

8. **Social Media Can Raise Our Anxiety Level and Change Our Self- perception.**
Unfortunately, we often turn to social media for acceptance whether it is the number of likes we receive or the comments that our pictures or opinions receive. I watch people consumed by a screen engaged in impersonal interaction instead of communicating with another person. Take regular breaks from all your social networks. Have face- to- face communication. If you feel emotions strongly like I do, you can be overwhelmed by everything that people reveal on

social media. I am also a helper, so the minute someone states a problem I want to help.

9. **Find The Knowledge You Need.**
We all have different strengths and weaknesses. Just because you may lack the skills to do something does not mean that you do not have something to offer. If you need to be better at something, research it, find a mentor and gain the knowledge. Use the skills you must improve and be grateful for what you can do instead of beating yourself up for what you have not yet learned. I learned this recently when I started guitar lessons. The first few lessons were difficult for me because I am a visual learner, and it takes time for me to process things. I have seen myself gradually improve and I can now do things that I never would have imagined in the beginning. You must keep a positive attitude and not be frustrated for this to work.

10. **Separate Constructive Criticism from Negative Noise**
Constructive criticism helps us grow while negative comments are destructive. When someone criticizes you and there is nothing to learn from the comment tell yourself that you are only hearing one voice. Everyone can have an opinion, but it might not always be accurate. When the criticism is helpful take some time to absorb it because even constructive criticism has a sting. After you have taken it in decide how you can use the comments to improve.

11. **Realize That You Have Special Gifts to Offer.**
I often hear people say they do not have a special gift. They do not think they offer anything special to those around them, but these people are inevitably the ones who offer the most without even realizing it. Think for a moment and ask yourself what your gift is. In case you are having trouble coming up with an answer, here are some possible gifts that you may be giving without thinking about it.

- **Strong faith** I know several people who have not had an easy life, but instead of being bitter and asking, "Why me?" they trust completely in God's plan, and feel that God will provide what they need to make it through any hardship. Faith like that is inspirational because many people will claim a belief in God until something goes wrong. It takes a strong faith to carry on in his name no matter what test is put before you. When people show this faith:, they are gifting others with peace and hope. Leave your worries at his feet and do your best to be the best.

- **Gifts of food:** Food can lift your spirits and giving food is an act of love. If you know someone who is struggling, bring over a meal, and watch their face light up.

- **Compliments:** We could all probably find something negative and positive about everyone around us. I choose to look for the positive and I also choose to comment on it. We all need a little ego boost now and then, so hearing that we did a good job, or another positive point can encourage us.

- **Guidance:** At some point, everyone needs some advice and a little guidance to get back on track. It's probably best to wait until someone asks for your advice unless you must step in.

- **Joy:** Happy people are like magnets, they are fun to be around. They can see the positive in everything, and the laughter is contagious.

- **A strong spirit:** I love being inspired by the people who refuse to let circumstances keep them down. Whether they are struggling with physical, personal, or financial hardships, they keep getting back up and fighting with everything they must achieve their goals.

- **Being present:** This is one of the greatest gifts and sometimes difficult to give. At my school, the students often want to come in before or between classes to talk. Although there are always a zillion things that need to be done, I will put everything down and focus on them every time because I think it is more important. Our children often want us to be with them, and as mine grow older I find that I do not care what we are doing, I only want to spend time with them.

Of course, there are the gifts that we think of first, like being able to sing like an angel, draw like Michelangelo, or dance like Misty Copeland, but the everyday gifts are as important and as needed as the gifts that make someone a standout. Use your gifts generously and be amazed at the difference you can make.

12. **Seek Inspiration to Motivate You.**
    Seeing someone striving and thriving can motivate you to try harder to improve yourself. I am always more inspired by the people who persevere despite challenges. I love seeing the determination to succeed despite the odds. Don't forget that you may be someone else's inspiration. Realize you may have been afraid to do a three-mile run because you are overweight but by doing it how many other people can you inspire to do the same thing? I met a man named Maurice at a race and I will never forget him. Maurice had a rare condition that caused fluid to build on his brain. He had already had fifteen operations to drain the fluid. He told me he did races to show his daughters that anything was possible. Anytime I want to make an excuse about not running, I think of Maurice.

13. **Replace Negative Self-Talk with Positive Words.**
The next time you hear yourself saying something negative about yourself, replace it with a positive sentence. Have a mantra that you can repeat to fight self-doubt. A mantra doesn't even have to be an entire sentence. You can repeat something like "Strong, smart, invincible". I often think of a YouTube video where a father has his daughter repeat positive statements on the way to school. "I am a strong, intelligent girl. I am wonderfully made. I am God's child. I will do great things today." What a great way to prepare your child for the day. We should do the same.

14. **Find Your Crew.**
Surround yourself with people who enjoy the same things you do and who understand you. Your crew has your sense of humor and thinks your quirks and eccentricities are perfectly normal. I have a group of running friends who think the same way I do. We see running distance as a challenge while others think it is crazy. We run in all kinds of weather and think it's fun. Our laughter and our time together are restorative. We share stories about family and work, challenges, and dreams. Our biggest common thread is our love of bacon and the realization that although we enjoy the run, the food we share after is the best part. My friends are there to help me heal when I feel like the rest of the world does not understand me.

15. **Keep Improving.**
Never feel as if you have reached your peak. You should always be trying to evolve into a slightly better version of yourself. Keep pushing yourself and stepping outside your comfort zone. I love to run. It has saved me mentally on many occasions. As an older runner, I often hear comments saying I need to be careful because of my age, but I want to keep finding new challenges. I started running ultra-marathons (a run longer than 26.2 miles) several years ago

and my husband became angry and we had to have one of those talks that all couples should have when you are operating on different frequencies. He said, "I'm worried you are going to hurt yourself." I replied, "I know my limits." To which he responded, "That's what I'm afraid of because I know you will slam as hard as you can against those limits." We talked it out and not only was I able to make him understand that I need new challenges, but I also convinced him to be my support at my next race.

16. **Adopt a Strong Mindset.**
Believe you are enough and that you are valuable to those around you. Fight frustration and give yourself grace when you struggle with something. Tell yourself that you will figure it out eventually. Positive self-talk is a lifesaver for me. Anytime I start to beat myself up for my imperfections, I stop and turn my thoughts from negative to positive. It makes a huge difference.

17. **Allow People to See Who You Are**
None of us are perfect and often our imperfections are endearing. Drop any pretense of trying to be someone you are not and be comfortable being authentic. A false front can be exhausting to maintain. I always tell myself that as long as I am doing everything to the best of my abilities and in a spirit of love, it will all work out. When I first started working at the Christian school where I teach, I was sure they would discover that I was not Christian enough to be there, so at the end of the first year before we signed contracts, I spoke with our headmaster and told him I did not have all the scriptures memorized and I wasn't sure I was good enough to be there. He told me that he wanted teachers who would treat people like Jesus would like them to be treated, not someone who had just memorized verses. If I had not been open, I would have continued to worry.

18. **When We Are Transparent Others Follow Our Lead**
    When you are open about your struggles the people around you will be relieved and start to tell their own stories. Being transparent can not only release the burden you are carrying, but it can also make others more comfortable. It allows people to feel they are not alone in their struggles. My family has a few issues that most people would like to keep hidden in the back of a very dark closet, but when I started to openly talk about them, I was surprised everyone else had similar stories.

19. **Dare to be Different.**
    I often see people imitating someone they admire. They might copy a hairdo, a style of dress, or take up similar hobbies. Dare to be your own person instead of being a carbon copy of someone else. Imagine how tiring it must be to always try to fit a mold instead of being comfortable with who you are. I used to worry about saying the wrong thing and ruining someone's impression of me, but now my attitude is I have to be myself whether someone else approves of that or not.

20. **The Haters in Your Life Have Less Ammunition When You Admit Your Shortcomings.**
    If you already admit your weaknesses and you are comfortable with them, it isn't any fun for someone to attack you because you are not giving them the satisfaction of an emotional reaction. A moment I will never forget is when my niece, her friend, and I were on a moving sidewalk in the metro in Paris. Coming towards us on the other side were three French boys who started laughing at us. Instead of feeling upset that someone was mocking us, Cathy, my niece said something funny about herself and we started laughing. The three boys suddenly looked slightly ashamed. Don't let the bullies win. Love, laughter, and a sense of self will win every time.

21. **People Are More Comfortable Around You When You Are Yourself.**
    When someone is open about strengths and faults, we say that he is comfortable in his skin. Someone who can accept his faults can also accept the faults of someone else and people can sense this. I know not everyone is going to like me, but that is their choice, and I would rather let everyone know who I truly am than worrying about maintaining a pretense.

22. **Being Transparent Can Help You to Grow.**
    If you know your shortcomings, you also know what you need to do to improve. Once you are honest with yourself about imperfections you can start to work on growth. I have also found that if you express to others what your weaknesses are people are usually willing to help you improve. At one time, I owned a small bookstore. When I was at the town hall registering my business, I confessed to the woman that I had no idea what I was doing. She told me about a program in the town that matched new business owners with a mentor. My mentor gave me more help and information than I could have imagined, and if I had not have spoken up our relationship would never have happened.

23. **Communication Has to Go Both Ways to Be Effective.**
    Listening is one of the most important skills we use, but most of us do not do it well. Most of the time someone is waiting for a chance to interrupt instead of listening for understanding. Listening to people makes them feel appreciated and valued because someone is interested enough in them to take the time to listen. Listening skills can enhance any relationship. Listening helps maintain good communication, and this eliminates mistakes and misunderstandings. We could all communicate so much better if our listening skills were stronger.

24. **Give Your Listener Your Undivided Attention**
We all have a million things to do and it is difficult to put them down when someone wants to talk with us, but listening fully to someone can boost productivity in other ways. When we try to work while speaking with someone it sends the message that we don't want to speak to them and what they have to say doesn't matter. It is a better idea to make everyone feel special and valued. Your job will be much easier when you need to ask for help.

25. **When You Have a Conversation, Do Not Try to Top the Other Person's Troubles or Switch to a Story About You.**
Sometimes people only need to release their burdens. Look the person in the eye and pay attention. Let the person know that every word being said is important to you. Let the person you are speaking with have the spotlight instead of interrupting or making it be about you. This is difficult for me because I always think the person will feel better if he knows someone else experienced the same thing, but most of the time it's better to not make it about you.

26. **Ask Questions About What You Are Hearing.**
Not only does this show that you are fully engaged in the conversation, but also you will learn more about the topic you are discussing. Do not interrupt or jump to answer. Listen to what the person is saying and be patient while the speaker communicates a message. Sometimes silence makes people talk the most. I once ran a smoking cessation program at a local school. A boy had been caught smoking and sent to our group. Before we could even say anything to him, he said, "I don't have a problem. I could stop if I wanted. I only smoke a pack a day. Maybe I do have a problem. What do I do? No one ever interrupted and our silence allowed him to work through the problem himself.

27. **Don't Allow Your Emotions to Control Your Words.**
When we are trying to be heard and understood, frustration and anger can be major roadblocks. Work on controlling your emotions instead of saying things you will later regret. I usually take a deep breath to let any initial feelings calm down before I speak. Before you begin your argument, acknowledge the other person by saying "I understand what you are saying." My daughter and I went through a difficult time when she was seventeen because we spoke with our emotions. Now we try to hear each other.

28. **You Can Change Someone's World with Your Words.**
As a teacher, I know how powerful my words can be. I teach teenagers and this age is a roller coaster ride of emotions. My prayer each day is that I only lift people up and that I do not say anything by mistake and tear someone down. I love when students tell me I make them feel loved or smart. You will be amazed at the power you hold in your words. Use them for good. My favorite example of this is when one of my students was talking to another student about all the different hair extensions the student would wear. I said I was sure she was also beautiful without the extensions. I didn't realize the extensions were a symbol of her attempt to fit the standards of beauty. The next day she came in and pulled off her wig revealing her real hair. I looked at her and said, "You see, you are beautiful without them." She never had extensions again. She is content in her natural beauty.

29. **Let Others into Your Space.**
I have learned that sometimes my students need a hug, a chance to describe the day, or a minute to regroup with someone they trust. Adults are the same. Most people want a chance to tell their stories. Being accessible and available to others can turn people's lives around. Sometimes my youngest will come downstairs and sit on the sofa in my office. That is my clue that she wants to talk or to be with

me. Most of the time all you have to do is be present. I have a student who is a high achiever, driven, and easily frustrated because she has overextended herself. She came into my classroom during a break and said, "Madame, your room makes me feel calm and peaceful. I need to sit here for a few minutes." I hope I can always provide that type of space.

30. **Relationships Should Be a Top Priority.**
    We all need a variety of communities in our lives to nurture us. Our interactions with others drive everything we do. We need support from family and friends to encourage us in our endeavors. If we have strong connections at work, we can be more productive and connections in general can create amazing opportunities. I met the mayor of my town through an article I had written. He introduced me to some of the town leaders and helped me join the local business organization to help promote my writing. He has also come to my school to help the teacher who teaches a leadership class. You never know where your next connection might lead.

31. **Time Is One of the Crucial Elements of a Good Relationship.**
    When my first child was born, I was so worried about being a good parent, but I learned that one of the most important things to do was to spend time with each other and to work at making memories. Last year I decided to switch to working part-time. I spent time going to lunch with my children, talking with my family on the front porch and generally getting to know my family again. I will be going back full-time this year and when I told my youngest, she looked distressed. I had to assure her that I would have plenty of time to spend with her. The next time your friends want to do something special, but you brought homework, go with your friends. Those relationships will probably bring you more joy.

32. **Show an Interest in the People in Your Circle.**
    It is so easy to become consumed with yourself. You want to talk about your day, and you want someone to understand your emotions. If you find that many of your conversations, are one sided with you doing all the talking, it may be time to show some interest in your loved ones. Ask friends and family questions about themselves. It cannot always be about you. The quickest way to make someone feel special is to ask them questions about themselves. When you do ask the questions make sure you listen to the answers. How many times has someone said, "How are you?" And as you are answering they turn away to speak with someone else?

33. **Know That Friendship Should Be Quality Not Quantity.**
    It doesn't matter how many friends you have; it matters how good they are. When hard times hit which friends are still around? Which friends do you feel comfortable with no matter what you are doing, and which ones can you still be comfortable with in silence? Everyone deserves at least one person who understands you completely, who can finish your sentence, and who loves everything you do. One person like that is worth fifty fair-weather friends.

34. **Always Love Fully.**
    When you love fully you are opening yourself up to pain and a wide range of emotions, but a life where love is not given and felt passionately is not complete. Love is a healer, and with all the hurt in the world, love can be the difference maker. React in love and you cannot go wrong. Showing love makes you vulnerable to hurt and pain, but it also fills you up as nothing else can. I have had my share of hurt, betrayal, and disappointment in the love arena, but a commitment I made to myself early in life is no matter how much someone I love hurts me, and how long it takes me to recover, I will always believe that loving with all my being is the most important thing I can do, and trying to feel less or

put my defensives up will only be half of what I could experience.

35. **Sometimes You Must Let a Relationship Go.**
As hard as it is to accept, certain relationships are toxic for us. All relationships involve a give and take, some compromise, and some work, but it is time to step away when the emotions are stressful or destructive. It may be someone who was once your best friend or a family member, but some relationships will only hurt you and cannot be healed. Go through a mourning period for that relationship and then move on and let it go. There is nothing healthy about rehashing the same ugly scenario. Chalk it up to another lesson learned and prepare for the next amazing person to enter your life.

36. **It Is Important to Be Part of a Community.**
Communities come in many different forms, but the common thread is that you can feel a part of a greater group and you can reach out for support and advice. When life becomes difficult, having a support group can make all the difference. When you are a part of a community that feels like family, the burden that you are carrying can be made lighter when others are there to help you. I have a group of friends that I call my prayer warriors. Whenever anyone needs some extra prayers, they are there. We make each other laugh until our stomachs hurt, and we would help each other in any situation. Feeling supported and loved makes the harder days easier.

37. **Every Day You Have a Chance to Make a Connection.**
Have you ever had someone tell you that something simple you did made a huge difference? You never know how something you do or say might make a connection with someone who needs it. God puts connections in front of us all the time. It could be something that someone says that sparks a light and makes us see what has remained hidden

from us. It could be a person who shows us a dream is possible or inspires us to be better. I know that some people think they don't have anything worthwhile to help someone make it from one point to another, but you never know how a small gesture can change everything.

38. **Be a Mentor.**

Do you have a skill you can teach? There is need everywhere for knowledge and experience. If you have woodworking skills, you could help with Habitat for Humanity building homes, and you can teach others how to build. If you own a small business, offer a workshop on how to start a business or sign up to mentor a new business owner. Check with the local YMCA, church, and local organizations to find a spot where your expertise can be used. If you pass your knowledge on, you can help someone else find the same success that you have had.

39. **Do Acts of Kindness.**

I warn you that these are slightly addictive. Once you do one, you will want to continue. I am going to commit to at least one act of kindness a day for this year. I truly believe that blessings that you give out, come back to you, so be prepared to be blessed. You never know when an action that you think is simple, could be the bridge that someone needed. My daughter and I were in McDonald's and an older man was behind us in line. I still had my debit card out and I noticed that he was fumbling for money, so I moved over and slid my card through the machine to pay for his meal. He was so thankful, and he told me his wife had been sick and today she wanted to come out for breakfast. He brought us over to meet her and I told her I hoped she felt better. The man pulled out three red stones and gave them to us. He told us they were blessing stones and if we kept them with us our lives would be full of blessings. I carry them everywhere I go.

40. **Be The Sail, Not the Anchor in a Relationship.**
    If I think of a negative person in my life, I can feel my mood dip, and a weight descends on me. This type of person drains my energy, and feels like an anchor pulling me down. I like to help people, so when someone comes to me with a problem, I listen, and then I offer some solutions. I can instantly tell the difference between someone who is truly in need of some help, and is looking for a solution, and someone who wants to wallow in misery. The first, I can help, the second, I cannot. A positive person is like a sail because there is always an attitude of anything is possible. Although this person may sometimes have bad days, the reaction is always that tomorrow will be better. This person inspires you and makes your day a little brighter. Both attitudes are contagious, and both will affect your life, so choose which type you want around you. We cannot always manage to avoid the anchors in our lives, but we can limit the time we spend with them. Our lives are too short to let toxic people drag us down, so try to seek out the sails in your life.

41. **Any Relationship is a Give and Take.**
    There will be highs and lows and a good relationship requires communication, trust, and a sense of humor. Life is too short to be surrounded by people who tear you down, manipulate you, do not have your best interests in mind, and generally make you miserable. Surround yourself with people who make you laugh and encourage you. My husband loves me despite my many faults. We are partners and although we do not always agree we respect each other's opinions, and we support each other completely. We both know the signs of when one of us needs some quiet time to renew from what life is throwing at us. We are opposites in both personalities and likes, except that we both think each other is the best human around.

42. **Positive Attitudes Attract People to You.**
When someone can see the positive side to a situation or find humor in a negative it helps those around you. Suddenly a problem that looked like a mountain seems solvable. Negativity can weigh people down while positivity can lighten the load. I have a student who can find the positive in anything. You can throw the most negative scenario at her and after thinking for a moment she will find the light. The fact that she can do that makes me stop when I find myself starting to be negative. Positive attitudes can lighten the mood and help someone who is struggling feel better.

43. **Be Ready to Forgive.**
Love is forgiveness. When someone we love lets us down or worse, betrays us in some way, it is easy to carry around bitterness. This only causes us added stress. Address the situation with the person involved, communicate your feelings, and evaluate if the relationship can be salvaged or if it is time to step away. My son is wired very differently than me. He is focused on the present and doing one thing at a time while I am dwelling on the past, excited about the future, and trying to do as much as possible in the present. He never comes to visit us and it has hurt me and I have spent too much time wondering why. At one point I had the reaction of a two-year old and I told myself that I wouldn't contact him until he contacted me. Of course, I realized that would not be acting in love, so I regularly reach out to show my love.

44. **Understand Before Reacting.**
There are so many situations where our first reaction is to become angry, but we need to take a moment before we react to try to fully understand what is happening and what is behind a person's actions. Many times, we can defuse a situation by reacting with love or humor. It can potentially turn a bad situation into a positive one. Before you react, ask

what has caused the words or actions. A student came in late to my class one day and I told her in an exasperated voice that I was marking her late and then I continued the class. I found out later that she had been in a bad car accident on the way to school. I should have given her a chance to explain. I went and found her and gave her a bear hug and an apology.

45. **No one Has to Settle for Unhappiness.**
We can change anything we want when we are ready to make the change. Everyone has the choice to decide how to react to a situation and it is within your grasp to decide what path you wish to follow. Have you ever heard someone complain about something in life that is possible to change and then the person begins to tell you all the reasons he is locked into misery? You must leave the excuses at the door and take a step towards the life you deserve.

46. **There is Always Someone Else Who Has Bigger Problems Than You.**
When you start to realize this, you will become more grateful for the good things in your life. Put your problems aside and see if you can help someone else. A few kind words or a simple smile can do amazing things to turn around someone's day. We start our classes with prayer requests, and I am always amazed at the burdens that people are carrying. I have a sign in my class that says, "You have no idea what the person next to you is dealing with, be kind always."

47. **Make a List of What You Want from Life.**
Do not put any restrictions on it. Do not say, "Well, I would like this, but it isn't possible." Write down everything you want. Now devise a plan for how you are going to make it happen. Anything is possible, but we are often the ones holding ourselves back because of fear. My oldest sister had always wanted to go to France and one day she told me she

knew she would never be able to go. At the same time, I attended a conference where the speaker said, "Imagine something you would like to do, but something is getting in the way, whether it is money or something else. Go sit for thirty minutes and figure out how you are going to do it." I sat down and figured out a budget and a way to take my sister and my two older children to France. Sometimes it takes sitting down and figuring out how to make it work.

48. **Have a Fearless Attitude.**
I admire people who say, "Why not?" and take all kinds of risks. It has always been a difficult mindset for me because I am so practical. I have to plan everything out and weigh all the risks, but I see the benefit of trying something without worrying about failure. We lose out on so many opportunities when we are hesitant to take the plunge. I want my students to learn this attitude, so I occasionally come up with activities that seem over the top and then I pray that it works! So far, so good!

49. **Being Stressed and Overwhelmed Is a Choice.**
Everyone at one time or another feels overwhelmed. There is not enough time in the day at work to plan, comfort, counsel, fill out paperwork, and answer e-mails. Oh, and we have to have a personal life as well. It is easy to feel stressed and overwhelmed with a crazy schedule, but you can choose not to feel that way. Here are some ways to deal with a busy schedule.

- **Do mission critical**

    When you have limited time to do things, do those things that are the most important first. Ask yourself what you have to finish for the next day. When you are feeling overwhelmed, it is not the time to try to work on the presentation that you are making in 2 months.

- **Use empty time effectively**

    Do work while waiting at the dentist, work on plans in your mind while you are in traffic. Brainstorm while you are in yet another meeting.

- **Make a list**

    We often think that we have so many things to do but once we write it down it seems more manageable, and it can also keep us from forgetting things. Cross things off as you complete them.

- **Be in the moment.**

    Whatever you are doing, be there fully. While you are working do not try to multitask. When you are with your family, be with them completely. If you try to do ten different things at once, you will not do any of them well.

- **Have some fun.**

    I know you are thinking that you do not have time for fun, but the truth is you will be more productive if you take some time from you. You will feel more renewed and less burnt out. Set some guidelines such as I will work until ten and then 10-11 is my time.

50. **Failure Has a Nasty Sting but It Makes You Stronger.**
    It is never fun to fail at something, but it has taught me some very valuable lessons. The greatest lesson I have learned is that failure is the first step towards greater success. It has also taught me that I should not be ashamed of falling short if I keep trying to make it right. Failure is emotional and painful, but it makes us better and wiser. My greatest sense of failure was with karate. I trained for six years and although it was very difficult both physically and mentally, I learned so many valuable lessons. My problem was that you often have to do multiple motions at the same time, but my

body often has trouble even focusing on one! I discovered that through practice you can persevere so I always try to control frustration and tell myself that I will eventually learn what I am trying to master.

51. **Accept That Most People Who Witnessed Your Failure Probably Moved on Five Minutes After It Happened So You Should Too.**
We are often embarrassed by our failures, and we worry about what people will think of us, but most people are too wrapped up in their own business to be worried about us. Cover the issue with a positive attitude and move on. I often wish I had. There have been numerous times when I have mentioned an incident that was weighing heavy on me, and I realize the person cannot even remember the moment.

52. **A Good Sense of Humor is A Powerful Weapon to Yield Against Failure.**
If you can laugh at your problems, you have already won your battle. You can also win people over to your side when they see how well you are reacting to a setback. It shows that you are confident that everything will be o.k. I like using my situations to help someone else deal with a struggle. It makes it easier to find humor and react positively when you feel that your experiences can help someone else.

53. **Breathe and Believe.**
There are times when discouragement will wash over you and the best thing you can do is to take a deep breath and believe that the outcome will be positive. There is powerful truth in saying that sending out powerful, positive thoughts makes things happen. Give yourself some grace and tell yourself that you will figure out each issue as it comes. One of the best students I have ever had would become discouraged when she did not think she was performing well. One day when she was having a meltdown, I walked over and

said, "Why do you let it defeat you? Figure out what you did wrong and then try again until it is easy for you."

54. **Take a Break**
There are times when we become overwhelmed, or fatigue saps our creativity. Taking a break to regroup and coming back later when we are renewed can make all the difference. I have had so many times when I felt I had hit a wall and then when I came back the problem resolved itself in minutes. Sometimes we need some time to shake the cobwebs out.

55. **Set Reachable Goals.**
Set some goals for success for whatever you are trying to achieve. Make them attainable and measurable and applaud yourself as you achieve each one and give yourself grace and regroup when you fall short. Goals will motivate you and push you to stretch yourself a little further. I have had a goal for the past few years of running at least one thousand miles a year. I track my weekly and monthly progress. My goal helps to motivate me because I have to write my progress down.

56. **Frustration Is A Waste Of Time**
When something isn't going our way, it is easy to have a meltdown, but that reaction does not help us to be better. Frustration keeps us from figuring out how we are going to break through the wall. We need to find out what is holding us back and then make a plan to improve our skills. Karate taught me that I can learn to do anything if I practice a lot and practice patience. There were so many times that I saw the experts show us how to do something and I would be thinking that I would never be able to do that, but eventually, I always figured it out.

57. **Excuses Are Your Failure Safety Net.**
Some people will come up with every excuse in the book why they cannot do something while others are willing to give something a try even if success is not guaranteed. The people who don't make excuses are willing to try new things that might carry some risk because they realize the results will lead to growth and improvement. The excuse-makers use the excuses as a shield to hide behind, but the problem with that is they are missing out on possibilities.

58. **Be Honest About What Went Wrong.**
Don't try to sugarcoat your failure. Be honest about the reasons and reflect on what you should have done differently. Do not rehash the event trying to look for righteousness. Accept that you stumbled and find out how you can avoid doing it again. Feeling sorry for ourselves is wasted time. I had offered to do something for someone but because I had too much to do, I found myself rushing the job for the friend and cutting corners so I could be finished faster. The final product was awful because I rushed, I was embarrassed, and I had to redo the project. I had to be honest with myself that If I had done it correctly the first time, I would have saved myself a lot of trouble.

59. **Be Open to New Possibilities.**
We have the power to welcome things and people into our lives and sometimes we block these new possibilities. Sticking with what we see as routine and safe is easier to do even though it may not be fulfilling. We have to be open to stepping outside of our comfort zone to try something new and to reach for something better. I had always thought that running more than a marathon distance was beyond my ability. One of my friends mentioned that her husband ran a local ultra-marathon and that it was fun. I decided to try it but I was so nervous because it was way out of my comfort zone. I enjoyed my first experience, and I asked the veteran

runners questions about how to train and fuel. Each ultra I learned a little more and now they are my favorite race. If you step out of your comfort zone you never know what amazing experiences, you might have.

60. **We All Have Demons in Some Form.**
It is what holds us back from being 100% happy or successful. It is often something we know we need to change, but it has a powerful hold on us. The demon can be in the form of the misuse of money, substance abuse, depression, and many other possibilities. It can also be a person we know is toxic for us, but for some reason, we just keep holding on to the relationship and incurring more battle wounds. My mother's demon was cigarettes. She grew up in a time when almost everyone smoked and when she finally realized the toll it was taking on her health, she was unable to stop. She was diagnosed with emphysema and had to always have an oxygen tank with her. It was difficult to see my active, fun- loving mother slowly die from a demon she could not defeat.

61. **Admit You Have a Demon.**
The first step in defeating your demons is admitting you have one. You cannot be in denial or make excuses about something that is holding you back. You have to see it for what it is and find the determination and motivation to remove it from your life. Don't worry about judgment from others if they discover you are struggling. This is about improving your life. Making excuses is a demon. If you imagine a better situation for yourself but then hear yourself making excuses why it cannot happen, you may have two demons to fight.

62. **Find The Support You Need.**
If you are struggling with a particular demon, you need to know you are not alone. Everyone has a dark corner in life, so do not feel that you cannot conquer this struggle. Ask for

help from an expert or someone you trust. Find a support group in your area. My husband is a recovering alcoholic. He had tried to stop several times, but he kept slipping back to his old habits. He finally had to ask for professional help.

63. **Make The Necessary Changes.**
Eliminating our demons often means making changes to our behavior, environment, or friend group. You cannot continue to put yourself in situations where you are tempted by your demons. Eliminate the triggers that cause your problems. I had a friend who abused food. She was going through a difficult time in her life, and she was using food to comfort herself. She went to see a nutritionist who advised her about what she should have in her grocery cart and told her to clean her cabinets of any food that was unhealthy or which she could not control the portion sizes

64. **Prayer is Powerful.**
Prayer is powerful hope. Prayer offers calm where there may be chaos. I have seen prayer chase away some strong demons, and you have nothing to lose by trying it. If you are not sure how to pray, start by welcoming Jesus into your life and asking for help and guidance. I have a group of prayer warriors who I ask for prayers. They prayed twice for situations involving a biopsy and cancer, once for me and once for my sister, and both times the doctor determined there wasn't even a need for a biopsy.

65. **Be Thankful for Your Scars.**
Those less than perfect moments in life when our demons rise up make us want to retreat somewhere safe where we will never be hurt again. The problem with that is we would miss out on a lot of wonderful moments as well. Life is meant to be full of emotions. It is raw and scary, but also beautiful and fulfilling. We cannot find that out though unless we are brave enough to jump in with both feet. We need an attitude that when life knocks us down, we need to get back up and

realize with each chink in our armor, we have one more story to tell and one more experience to provide us with wisdom.

66. **Our Health is a Factor in Every Area of Our Lives.**
    If our weight is out of control, we cannot be as active as we might need to be, especially if we have children. Excess weight also puts stress on our bodies. Stress management is also crucial to our health. Refusing to take care of your health will also hurt your family, so if you cannot see a need to improve your health for yourself, imagine what your family life will be like if you are in poor health. Don't ignore the warning signs your body is sending you. Pay attention and find the motivation to improve both for yourself and for your family.

67. **Find The Quiet.**
    Even the most outgoing, positive, sociable person needs a quiet place to escape from time to time. You can turn your commute in the morning into a chance to listen to music, reflect, or bask in the quiet. Books are the ultimate escape. You can jump into the fantasy of a story and leave everyday life behind. Being outside is therapeutic. Whether you go for a walk, sit on your porch, or swing in a hammock, taking in the beauty around you is calming. One of my favorite ways to renew is to go out on our porch and listen to the sounds of the neighborhood. It is a time when I don't have to answer a question or solve a problem. I can renew in other ways as well whether I take a walk, read, write, cook, or do something else that is soothing. When I make this renewal a regular practice, it changes my attitude towards everything else I do. Silence can be such a blessing sometimes. When there is silence, I hear the most. I can listen to all the thoughts swirling around in my head, and It is easier to reflect, and problem solve. Silence brings a feeling of peace because in that silence, it is possible simply to be present.

Being silent can help you find out important details about family, friends, and colleagues. Instead of replying immediately when someone makes a statement, be silent. The other person will fill the space with more information. You just need to have the patience to wait instead of interjecting. Silence has also been shown to offer health benefits that boost overall well-being. Silence helps lower blood pressure, which can help prevent heart attack, and boost the body's immune system. Noise has a physical effect on the brain, which can lead to elevated levels of stress hormones. Silence can release tension in the brain in just 2 minutes. Mindfulness is a word we hear related to good health, and it is achieved through silence.

68. **Movement is a Must.**

    My friends will not think I wrote this unless I mention that running for me is the ultimate healer. When I am running, I feel such a sense of peace, as if any stress is just falling off behind me. I can work out problems, generate ideas or simply listen to music. Running is what I turn to first when my emotions are out of balance. If running is not your sport choose anything that is an active activity.

69. **Music is a Healer.**

    Music can match your mood if you are feeling down or pensive and it can rev you up when you need motivation. Music soothes our soul and gives us a chance to sing along at the top of our lungs while we occasionally change the words. I have a song that I always listen to if I am stressed. The song begins and I can feel my whole-body relaxing. The right words encased in a melody can speak to us better than any other message.

70. **Spending Time with Animals Is Good Therapy.**

    Spending time with animals has always been a good way to decompress for me. Animals love you completely and they crave spending time with you. Our next-door neighbor has a dog that acts as if he is over the moon excited to see you to the point that he will start to howl, and even though I know he acts that way to almost everyone, it still lifts my spirits.

71. **Cooking is a Healthy Pastime.**
Cooking has always been a way to relax for me. Making good food and filling the house with wonderful aromas is always a pleasure. Have you ever noticed that when you have friends over everyone gravitates to the kitchen? Fill your life with good food and good friends to help you eat it. When the COVID virus hit my school went to virtual teaching. One day I had my classes cook with me and I taught them how to make French mayonnaise, an appetizer to use the mayonnaise, and French toast. Several parents told me that not only did the students want to cook more after our class, but it also gave them something to do as a family.

72. **Practicing Gratitude is an Important Exercise in Healing.**
List all the things you are thankful for, and any problems you encountered during the day start to fade away. Realizing all your blessings instead of focusing on burdens will make you feel better. Focusing on the blessings seems to attract more. When a friend's husband died from an accident, everyone would have accepted her to mourn her loss and although she did, she focused more on the memories they shared, the children they had, and the love he had given her. Those memories were like a blanket of comfort that she wrapped around herself.

73. **Sleep Can Solve Many of Our Problems.**
Sometimes the best answer to being worn out mentally and physically is to curl up and catch up on sleep. A good nap on a rainy day can make you forget any troubles you may have. I find that I become moody when I'm tired and I do not want to interact with people. I also know that my productivity level drops drastically when I am tired. A project that might have motivated me seems like a huge challenge if I am tired. I

also notice that I snack more when I am tired and weight gain has been linked to fatigue.

74. **Disconnect to Connect.**
We waste time checking for likes, searching for the right picture, scanning e-mail every five seconds, and taking another selfie. Our interactions have become impersonal swipes and taps. Technology can raise our anxiety level and keep us from spending time and focusing on the people we love. Set boundaries on how often you use your technology. Take back some of that time you are spending with a machine and use it for self-improvement. Listening to too much news can have negative effects. We are consuming what everyone else believes and we begin to question our own beliefs.

75. **Manage Stress.**
You are the only one with complete power over stress because you have a choice about how you react to situations and stress is never a good response. Pastor Joel Olsteen was speaking about stress when he said, "Instead of letting stress take over, be a person of excellence and find a calm, reasonable way to react." Show others what grace under pressure looks like and you are helping them defeat stress.

76. **Slow Down to Enjoy More.**
I know what it feels like when you are already late for work and as you turn onto the highway you realize the traffic is almost at a standstill. Letting your stress go through the roof is not going to help you arrive there faster. Relax and even let some people into traffic from their side streets. Listen to some great music and work through your day mentally. I can feel guilty that I am doing too much and guilty about not doing enough, but I do know that guilt is a useless emotion. Throw it out with the garbage. Slowness is not always easy for those of us who are driven, but I am trying to embrace

the positive aspects of slowing down a bit to enjoy the ride. Here are a few things to try to help you to slow down

- Sit somewhere comfortable. Close your eyes, breathe deeply, and imagine an ideal scene for you. Visualize something wonderful you want to happen.
- Pick up a great book and leave the world behind for a while as you explore a fantasy world or learn something new.
- Cook for pleasure. Cook because you want to, not because you have to. Cooking can be calming.
- Make a not- to- do list of tasks you can eliminate, or that someone else can do for you.
- Find an activity that makes you happy and feel the sense of relaxation wash over you.

77. **Rest and Food Make All the Difference.**
Most of the time when a child has a meltdown it is either because he is hungry or tired. The happiest child is one who has adequate rest and has a regular food routine. This does not change as we age. Remember the last time you started to become annoyed for no specific reason. Were you hungry or tired? Chances are the answer is yes. Rest and food keep us focused and productive and happy. My blood sugar drops quickly when I am hungry, and my mood will change on a dime. My family knows if I say I am hungry it is time to find mom a snack.

78. **Know What Fuels You.**
What do you need to be happy? I don't think it is something we take the time to think about, but it is so important to know what fills us and keeps us feeling fulfilled. My fuel comes from family, food, good books, writing, running, animals, and my students. Once you have your own list make sure you surround yourself with all those things. When

I have a bad day a trip to a bookstore, or an office supply store can turn my day around and make me smile again.

79. **Learn From Everyone.**
It doesn't matter where someone comes from, what they do in life, or how old they are because everyone can teach you something. If you approach life with your eyes open to this fact you will be amazed at what you will see. Even if you have experience with something someone might offer a fresh approach that will help you to move forward. Sometimes we need to see someone model a certain attitude or explain a different philosophy about something. Everyone has a potential lesson to offer so be ready to receive it.

80. **Laugh As Often as Possible.**
I often react to a horrible day with laughter. It seems like a comedy of errors when you have one of those days where one thing after another goes wrong. Laughter makes me feel better and it eases the tension of those around me. The sound of laughter can make you smile and lift your spirit. Laughter is contagious so be responsible for starting an epidemic.

81. **Change Your Focus.**
I would like to suggest that we could boost our energy level and generally improve our lives by changing our mindset. Instead of seeing our life as a burden full of things that we must do, what if we begin to intentionally look for the positive aspects of what we do daily? We could try to see what we have and do as blessings instead of burdens because when we are happy about something, we seem to find more energy and our step is lighter, but when we feel burdened it seems to sap our energy and pull us into a pity party. Our way of looking at our situation can not only change the outcome but can also relieve self-imposed stress. Take the way we view the workweek vs. the weekend. We look at work as the necessary evil that we have to do and we just try to make it to the weekend. We spend more time at work than

anywhere else so why do we not try to find some enjoyment in it instead of dreading it? What made you choose to work where you do? Who do you enjoy working with? Is there someone who benefits from your presence at work? What could you do to lift someone up at work?

- Every time you hear yourself forming a negative thought, force yourself to replace it with a positive. You wouldn't think that being positive would take work, but it is a mindset that needs to be practiced.

- When you start preparing for a pity party, look around you and start to count your blessings. Everyone is carrying burdens, but we often think ours is the heaviest until we really observe the people around us.

- Focus on something that makes you happy and think how lucky you are to be able to do that.

- Surround yourself with positive people and run away from the toxic. Negativity will drain the happiness out of you.

- Practice acts of kindness as often as you can. Put points in the blessing bank and the more you pour out blessings to others, the more you will receive in return.

Remember that every day is a choice where you are in control. Where will you place your focus? Will you be stressed, self-obsessed, and miserable or will you choose to motivate yourself and others? I choose to do my best to be a positive supplier of joy and to see the amazing blessings that are in front of me every day.

82. **Don't Lose Your Mind.**
What can be more important than our mental fitness? We spend so much time worrying about our physical appearance, but we often forget about the part of our body

that controls everything. Luckily there are some very easy strategies that we can follow to stay mentally sharp such as adequate rest, learning something new, being creative, doing puzzles and word games, reading, and teaching a talent to someone else.

83. **It's Not That Hard to Make Friends.**
Children do not care what someone does for a living or what color their skin is or what kind of car they drive. They enjoy each other's company, and they see each new child as a new chance to interact and have fun. Somehow as we become older, we make it so much more complicated. Start conversations with strangers at gatherings you attend, and you may be amazed at the connections you make. I was blessed to teach all four girls in a Nigerian family. When the oldest was married my husband and I were invited to the wedding. We only knew the family but instead of staying in the corner by ourselves we started talking to everyone and before long we were exchanging numbers and making wonderful contacts.

84. **Sharing What You Have Is Important.**
Most children like to at least show others the treasures they are carrying around if not share them. As parents, we are always telling our children how important it is to share what we have, but we often do not do it enough as adults. There is so much need around us that anyone who has the potential to share what they have should do so. One year at Christmas there was a teacher who did not have enough money to buy toys for her children. Another teacher and I bought toys and filled her workspace with them. Not only did her children have some toys, but she also felt our love.

85. **There Must Be Time to Play.**
A child knows the importance of play. Everyone needs time for fun and a chance to use creativity and imagination. As adults, we become too caught up in work and responsibility. Joy can be found in other places with other activities. Take

time every day to do something you enjoy. It doesn't matter how much work I have, if one of my children suggests that we do something together I am all in because when I retire work will disappear but I'm hoping my children will not.

86. **The Toys We Have Do Not Ensure Happiness.**
A child can have just as much fun with a box and some paper and crayons as he can have with the latest state- of- the- art gadget. Don't waste your money on the latest craze in an attempt to have the newest and the latest thing that everyone else has. I remember when my oldest had her first Christmas we had purchased as many toys for her as our budget would allow, but she left all the shiny things and amused herself for hours with the boxes they came in.

87. **Take The Time to Wander and Wonder.**
When did we become so busy that we cannot take in the wonder of what is around us? When you walk with a small child you must allow ample time to arrive at your destination because he will stop and marvel at every stone, plant, and insect along the way. Wander sometimes instead of going straight to your destination. I usually run for my exercise but yesterday I went for a walk. I saw so many beautiful flowers, stopped to pet a few dogs, and talked to some fellow walkers. Occasionally, it is better to slow down and see what is around us.

88. **They Never Worry About Time.**
Children never feel the need to hurry (unless candy or ice cream are involved.) Nothing is a waste of time because each activity deserves their attention. If we followed this habit our stress levels would drop significantly. I am always watching the clock and giving myself a certain amount of time to do each activity. Occasionally though I tell myself that I will take what the day offers without worrying about what I accomplish.

89. **What Needs to Be Thrown Out in The Trash?**
Sit down and do an honest evaluation of what will make you better and what is holding you back. Look at it as spring cleaning for your life. What clutter do you need to eliminate? What people do you need to move away from? What habits do you need to change? What things feel like burdens in your life? It is incredibly freeing to make positive changes that will improve your life.

90. **How Can You Improve Your Health?**
The obvious answers to that are to eliminate harmful substances and to reduce stress but there are other factors. You need to make sure you are eating well and engaging in physical activity. You also have to take care of your mental health. Last year I made the decision to only teach part-time because I was overwhelmed and exhausted. I didn't feel like I had time to breathe. After a year of doing that, my oldest child told me I was a different person. I was calmer and happier.

91. **You Need to Surround Yourself with People Who Will Make You Better.**
If the people you spend time with are partially responsible for any problems you have, you may have to stop spending time with them and find people who can help you live the life you deserve. This is an especially hard decision when the people dragging us down are family members.

92. **Learn to Say No.**
Everyone wants your time especially if you are good at what you do, responsible, and hard working. Do not feel guilty about guarding your time and balancing helping others and having time for yourself. I am terrible at saying no because I always want to help and I feel guilty if I don't. When I see a need, I want to help but the problem is that if you start doing too much you won't be good at any of it.

93. **Do What You Love.**
Our passions can fuel us and keep us energized. Doing what you love keeps you happy and motivated to succeed. Being passionate about something is contagious and attracts people to you. Positive people enhance your life and are often resources that you may need to move forward.

94. **Break Your Mold.**
It doesn't matter how many times you have tried to reach your dreams and failed or attempted to change something in your life without success. Change something you are doing and see if that makes a difference. Keep tweaking your routine until you figure out what is going to work for you. Create your own rules for success instead of following someone else's rules.

95. **Imagine More.**
Many people have very low expectations for their lives. They cannot envision some of the things that someone else takes for granted. What makes it difficult for someone to imagine more and not see the possibilities? Some of the problems might be due to low self-esteem, but most of the time the inability to imagine more is because of two things. If you can see the possibilities, you know you have to work to achieve them and making excuses about why you cannot is easier than putting in the work. The second reason is because many people cannot perceive themselves in certain situations. They limit themselves with their perceptions.

96. **Map Out Your Goals.**
Write out goals to improve your work, and your personal life. Detail what you want to achieve in the short term and long term and plan for how you are going to make it happen. Pick certain dates to revisit your goals. Mark the goals you have achieved with a green highlighter and reflect on what you need to do to move forward.

97. **Make a vision board.**
Put up images and photos that represent what you want to achieve in life. It could be for a job you would like to have or a house where you would like to live. This is just for you to dream, so think big. I write down all my expectations for the year. It is fun to revisit the board at the end of the year to see how many of your dreams come true.

98. **Ask God to open doors.**
I have found that my greatest blessings have come when I ask God to help guide me and to open the doors, I need to do his work. The doors are not always the ones I expected, but there always seems to be an amazing adventure waiting for me on the other side, if I am willing to step through.

99. **Nix Negativity.**
Every workplace has them. Those people who find fault with everything and everyone and feel the need to tell everyone about it. Why is it that negativity seems to be more powerful and destructive than a positive attitude? A certain amount of complaining is human nature. Everyone needs to vent from time to time, but negativity is not complaining when you are tired or overwhelmed. It is more of an attacking type of complaining where blame is placed on someone else. Negativity causes a myriad of problems.

In any workplace, gossip travels faster than any other form of communication. What someone says in the lounge or workroom will travel around the office like wildfire. When the complaints are heard by the person who is being attacked, nothing positive can come from the situation. One risks a confrontation at the least, and it probably ensures that there is now one less person who can be counted on to collaborate productively with the complainer on any future projects. It can also create an uncomfortable, strained relationship.

There is something about listening to criticism and negativity that makes you feel dirty and guilty. Negativity can pull your mood down faster than anything, and that feeling that you participated even by listening makes you feel guilty and unprofessional.

The complainers can be labeled as not being team players. If you associate yourself with someone who sows negativity, you can be labeled as not being a team player. You can lose respect from your co-workers because you are a problem finder, not a problem solver.

100. **Consistency Will Change Your Life.**

We all make plans to change certain things in our lives. We tell family and friends about how excited we are about the new changes we are going to make, and we begin working towards our new goal with passion. Unfortunately, the passion only lasts about a week and then we fall back into old habits only to try to restart about a month later and then again, we give up. If we all did more things in our lives consistently, we could turn our lives around dramatically. Consistency is the answer to changing everything. Here are some ways that consistency can help you.

- Be consistent exercising and you will change your body.

- Be consistent reading and you will improve your mind.

- Be consistently positive and you will bring good things into your life.

- Eat well consistently and you will have more energy and better health.

- Sleep consistently and you will improve your productivity and your focus.

- Practice excellence consistently instead of settling for average and you will be proud.

- Serving others consistently will improve your self-esteem.
- Finding good in others consistently will improve your character.
- Trying new things consistently will stimulate your brain.
- Budgeting your money consistently will ensure that you always have some.
- Learning on the job consistently makes you a better employee.
- Spending time consistently doing the things you love will make you happier.
- Spending time with friends consistently will make you more secure.
- Laughing consistently will make you happy.
- Staying abreast of current events consistently will make you knowledgeable.
- Smiling consistently will make those around you happy.
- Listening completely consistently will help more than giving advice.
- Being present consistently instead of thinking about the past or future will open your eyes.
- Taking a few minutes consistently to reflect can clear your mind.
- Follow your instincts consistently and make good decisions.
- Treating others with love consistently will bring love back into your life.

- Doing your best consistently means that you have done your best to improve.

101. **God Will Send You Who and What You Need.**
We spend so much time worrying about what our next step should be, or how can we make our situation better, but God is the one with the plan. Have you ever noticed that certain people entered your life right at the moment you needed them the most? Have you ever wondered if you filled that same need for someone else? So often all you need to do is ask for the blessing you are longing to have. If you do not receive it realize that it may not have been in your best interest.

Conclusion

I hope you have found some messages that ring true to you and that will help you in your life. Remember that being slightly broken makes you more interesting and being a little imperfect means you always have something you can be working on to improve. Here is a summary of some of the advice you can start to use right now.

- Change from an excuse maker to a challenge breaker.
- Come up with a plan that works for your happiness.
- Find a bulletin board and put up photos or images that represent your vision.
- Write a goal journal.
- Pick a day of the week and write down everything you are hoping to achieve that week.
- Read something inspirational.
- Seek guidance from someone you admire.
- Ask why not instead of saying I can't
- Avoid the dream crushers of negativity and fear.
- Focus on mending the brokenness around you by helping others and you will not notice your chips and dents quite as much.

About the Author

I recently retired from teaching after forty years. During that time, I have tried to balance my writing, my teaching, and my family life. Retirement is offering me the chance to spend more time with my writing and I could not be more grateful. Let me tell you about my passion for writing.

My years in the classroom have taught me lessons I have used in my writing. One of the things that teaching has taught me is that everyone needs some encouragement, even when life is full of blessings. I enjoy providing that encouragement for both my students and my readers. Teaching also taught me the importance of community and relationships. I hope I can help readers find the way to build the community and life they need to be happy.

Writing has always been an activity that gives me peace. I tell people I am usually smiling when I am writing. My specialties are parenting, running, education, and self-help. I self-published a teaching guide called *Stay Away from the Girl's Bathroom*. (The girl's bathroom at my school was where all the drama happened, so you entered at your own risk.) I write monthly essays for my local media in two magazines and our newspaper. I have been published in a variety of magazines from Trail Runner to Atlanta Parents. I have a blog that you can reach at www.jeniferswriting.org, a Pinterest page that is found at https://www.pinterest.com/jenniferbonn, and I can be found at medium.com.

Writing is something that I love to do, but it is also something I have to do. Once an idea is in my head I feel as if I will not be at peace until I put it into words. I think about it constantly until I can work it out into the proper form. Ideas come to me from something someone said, an article in the paper, or something I see. I often think of a great idea when I am out running, and I come in to write it on my board before I forget. I have a small whiteboard on my podium where I write thoughts for my writing. I own about fifty journals and they all have some writing in them. I prefer writing out my thoughts in the journals before typing them out. There is just something magical to me about the feel of paper and pen.

I am an avid runner and reader and although I have no idea what I am doing, I have fallen in love with gardening. I always love having flowers(especially roses) around me and I find I feel the same about being in a green space that I have helped create.

I am blessed with an amazing family that keeps me on my toes. I have three children of whom one has just finished her first year in college and is living with us. My oldest gave birth to our first grandchild three months ago and I am enjoying being a grandmother. My husband John is my biggest cheerleader and my voice of reason. We have been married forty years. We have a cat named lowkey who is so large he has to shimmy through the cat door and has made an art of napping anywhere.

My life is full of blessings and challenges and I hope you will enjoy reading my writing as I share all of them with you.

Bibliography

Anonymous (1989). *Keep it simple: Daily meditations for twelve-step beginnings and renewal.* New York: HarperCollins.

Brett, Regina. (2012). *Be the Miracle.* Hachette Book Group USA.

Frost, R. L., & Asselineau, R. (1966). *Robert Frost.* Paris: P. Seghers.

Goff, B. (2020). *Dream big: Know what you want, why you want it, and what you're going to do about it.*

Goff, B., & OverDrive, Inc. (2018). *Everybody, Always.* Place of publication not identified: Thomas Nelson.

Goff, B., Miller, D., & Hoopla digital. (2015). *Love does: [discover a secretly incredible life in an ordinary world].* United States: IDreamBooks Inc.

Goldberg, N. (1998). *Writing down the bones pocket classic: Freeing the writer within.* Boston, Mass: Shambhala.

Grenny, J., Patterson, K., Maxfield, D., McMillan, R., & Switzler, A. (2013). *Influencer.*

Greitens, E. (2016). *Resilience: Hard-won wisdom for living a better life.*

Honoré, C. (2009). *In praise of slowness: Challenging the cult of speed.* Pymble, NSW: HarperCollins ebooks.

Lewis, C. S. (2007). *Words to Live By: A guide for the merely Christian.*

Maxwell, J. C., & Dornan, J. (1997). *Becoming a person of influence.* Nashville, Tenn: Thomas Nelson Publishers.

Maxwell, J. C., & Maxwell, J. C. (2016). *Jumpstart your priorities: A 90-day improvement plan.*

Orloff, J., Fields, A., & Books on Tape, Inc. (2008). *Positive energy: 10 extraordinary prescriptions for transforming fatigue, stress, and fear into vibrance, strength, and love.* Santa Ana, Calif.: Books on Tape.

Osteen, J. (2021). *Empty out the negative: Make room for more joy, greater confidence, and new levels of influence.*

Nerburn, K. (2019). *Simple Truths: Clear and Gentle Guidance on the Big Issues in Life.* New World Library.

Skye, A., Lester, M., & Dean, C. (2012). *Self-care for life: Find joy, peace, serenity, vitality, sensuality, abundance, & enlightenment - each and every day.* Avon, Mass: Adams Media.

Readtrepreneur. (2018). *Summary: The wisdom of Sundays by Opray Winfrey.*

Silverstein, S. (2014). *The giving tree.*

Stephens, S., & Gray, A. (2009). *The worn out woman: When life is full and your spirit is empty.*

Index

acceptance, 22
animals, 28
attitude, 18
being different, 9
being present, 6, 12
being yourself, 10
breaks, 23
community, 15
compliments, 5
confidence, 1
consistency, 39
constructive criticism, 4
cooking, 29
crew, 7
demons, 25
depression, 25
disconnect, 30
emotions, 12
excuses, 24
failure, 21
faith, 5
fearlessness, 20
focus, 32
food, 5, 31
forgiveness, 18
friends, 34
friendship, 14
frustration, 8, 23
goals, 23, 37
God, 5, 7, 15, 38, 41
gratitude, 26, 29

guidance, 5
happingess, 19
harmful speech, 2
haters, 9
health, 27
honesty, 24
humor, 22
insecurities, 1
inspiration, 6
joy, 5
kindness, 16, 33
laughter, 32
limitations, 2
listening, 10–11
love, 14
making connections, 15
mentoring, 16
movement, 28
negative self-talk, 7
negativity, 38
Olsteen, J., 30
overwhelmed, 20–21
perfectionism, 1, 3, 8
play, 34
possibilities, 24
prayer, 26
problems, 19
quiet, 27
reacting, 18
reacting to others, 3
relationships, 13, 17

ending, 15
rest, 31
saying no, 36
self-esteem, 1, 7
self-improvement, 7
sharing, 34
show interest, 14
skills, 4
sleep, 29, 39

slow down, 30
social media, 3
special gifts, 4–6
spiritual strength, 5
stress, 20–21, 30
time, 13, 35
toys, 35
vision board, 38

www.ingramcontent.com/pod-product-compliance
Lightning Source LLC
Chambersburg PA
CBHW061514040426
42450CB00008B/1606